By Theresa Morin
Illustrations by Ron Wheeler

Once there lived a man named Moses. He was the one who led God's special people, the Hebrews, to a beautiful new land God gave them.

Moses knew that God loved His people, and he knew God had called him to be their leader. At first Moses didn't want such an important job, but his people needed him.

You see, for hundreds of years the Hebrews had been slaves to the Egyptians. They had to work all day in the hot, hot sun.

They made bricks to build cities. They grew food for the people and animals. Moses saw how tired and sad they were, and he wanted to set them free.

Then Moses heard God speak! God told Moses how to lead His people to freedom! Together they marched out of Egypt, right toward. . .

The sea? "God is leading us to the sea?" The
Hebrews were confused. "Why don't we head for
the hills where we can hide?"

Then they all stopped talking and listened. It couldn't be! But it was. From far away they could hear the beat of horses' hooves.

Pharaoh, the Egyptian ruler, was following them with his army. The Hebrews cried to Moses, "If Pharaoh finds us he will make us slaves again!"

Moses looked around. If they turned one way
they'd run into a tall mountain. If they went the
other way they would drop off a steep cliff.
Behind them were the Egyptians. And straight
ahead was the sea.

Moses had nowhere to look but up. He turned his eyes to heaven and prayed for God's protection from Pharaoh's mighty army.

Then Moses comforted the people. He promised them that God would fight their battle for them! They only had to trust. After all. . .

God had sent them a cloud by day to protect them from the hot sun and fire by night to light their way. And God had given them Moses to lead them!

With new strength, the Hebrews got back in line
and followed Moses. Moses didn't turn right.
And he didn't turn left.

He headed straight to the sea! God had told him to walk as far as he could on dry land, and then a path for the Hebrews would open up through the middle of the water!

Suddenly, Moses raised his rod and a great wind came up. As the people walked into the sea, it parted before them!

They were walking on dry land, just like you do every day, even though they were in the middle of the water. It was a miracle!

The Egyptians saw the sea part for the Hebrews. The Egyptians kept on chasing them, right down into the dry bed of the sea. But great waves crashed over the Egyptians.

They couldn't chase the Hebrews any more. The
Hebrews were no longer Egypt's slaves! They
were free.

When they reached the other side, the Hebrews praised God for saving them. And they thanked Moses for listening to God and obeying Him.